I0481207

The 20 Habits of Effective Women

Building habits that strengthen the woman's Personality, Influence, Confidence, Entrepreneur and Relationships.

Angelina Nelson

© **2021** Angelina Nelson Publishing

Summary:

Introduction:

What's the significance here to be an effective lady?
Does it include having a lucrative work?
Being monetarily free?
Claiming extravagant vehicles or maintaining your own business? Or then again is it basically having a solid family?
Accomplishing genuine satisfaction?
Finding your motivation or carrying on with a more significant life?
Everybody has various meanings of success, yet whatever it intends to you, there are sure propensities all fruitful individuals share that assist them with making progress both in their own and expert lives.
US organizations possessed by ladies are developing at a sensational rate. Be that as it may, ladies in business will in general face unexpected difficulties in comparison to their male partners, and are undeniably more averse to arrive at the million dollar mark. In view of an investigation of more than 750 ladies in business, this book subtleties a portion of the habits of highly successful female business visionaries—and how to copy their privileged insights for progress.

In the course of recent years, the quantity of organizations owned by ladies has developed by over 42%. Indeed, in 2008, this ladies claimed firms represented more than 1.9 trillion dollars in sales.

However, while an ever increasing number of ladies are anxious to turn out to be entrepreneurs, they're additionally as yet confronting a larger number of difficulties than men.

Organizations possessed by ladies are almost half more averse to arrive at the million dollar mark—and regularly produce less profit from speculation for quite a long time worked.

Success can be characterized from multiple points of view and obviously every one of the five kinds have their own meaning of accomplishment. Taken by and large, in the event that we think about business income and individual fulfillment with work/life balance.

In this book we'll mention the best 20 habits of effective women.

1) She focus on growth:

Maintaining a business is loaded up with a huge load of minor subtleties, the entire year. Be that as it may, we figured out how to actually remain zeroed in on the higher perspective: developing her business. This implies moving beyond the subtleties, the billable hours and the past due solicitations—and focusing on the way toward getting (and dealing with!) more business, in less time.

Knowledge is power, and a fruitful lady realizes that to prevail throughout everyday life, you should be knowledgeable. Regardless of whether it's ready to go or everyday life, an effective lady isn't hesitant to explore, set out to find out about new points and pose smart inquiries.

She puts forth an attempt to remain educated and cherishes learning new things. She realizes that there is something to be gained from everyone and if there's anything she doesn't totally comprehend, she'll make a special effort to instruct herself.

We'll explain in detail how you will do the methods for developing a growth mindset:

-Acknowledge and embrace imperfections: Hiding from your weaknesses means you'll never overcome them.

-View challenges as opportunities: Having a growth mindset means relishing opportunities for self-improvement.

-Try different learning tactics: There's no one-size-fits-all model for learning. What works for one person may not work   for you.
Replace the word "failing" with the word "learning": When you make a mistake or fall short of a goal, you have not failed; you've learned.

-Stop seeking approval: When you prioritize approval over learning, you sacrifice your own potential for growth.

-Emphasize growth over speed: Learning fast isn't the same as learning well, and learning well sometimes requires allowing time for mistakes.

-Place effort before talent: Hard work should always be rewarded before inherent skill.

-Highlight the relationship between learning and "brain training": The brain is like a muscle that needs to be worked out, just like the body.

-Learn from other people's mistakes: It's not always wise to compare yourself to others, but it is important to realize that humans share the same weaknesses.

-Make another objective for each objective achieved: You'll never   be finished learning. Since your midterm test is over doesn't mean you should quit being keen regarding a matter. Development disapproved of individuals realize how to continually make new objectives   to keep themselves animated.

-Ponder time and exertion: It takes some effort to learn. Try not to hope to dominate each subject under the sun at a time.

-Take ownership over your attitude: When you build up a development attitude, own it. Recognize yourself as somebody who has a development attitude and be glad to allow it to direct you all through your instructive vocation.

2) She challenges herself :

A successful lady doesn't get comfortable the dreariness of everyday life. She is continually making progress toward additional in every part of her life whether actually or intellectually and is continually driving herself higher than ever. She acknowledges demands with certainty and follows them with courage, setting the bar much higher each time.

Challenges are a piece of regular daily existence. They make us more grounded and without them life turns out to be to some degree trivial in light of the fact that we don't have anything to think about the great occasions to. These challenges come in numerous structures.

For a few, the test is accomplishing admirably grinding away, for other people, it is having the chance to grasps with monetary concerns.

Yet, paying little heed to the test, looking up to it is vital. Doing so will cause you to feel like you can deal with yourself, it will likewise cause you to comprehend the estimation of what you have now. It's genuinely captivating how effective ladies approach issues.

Where others see invulnerable hindrances, they see difficulties to embrace and deterrents to survive.

Their trust despite difficulty is driven by the capacity to relinquish the pessimism that holds such countless in any case reasonable individuals back. Success isn't the solitary thing dictated by your attitude. Positive thinkers charge better; they treat disappointment as learning encounters and accept they can improve later on.

The principal thing you should do is quit considering difficulties to be issues, yet begin considering them to be openings. On the off chance that you had a decision, you would most likely look to dodge difficulties. Be that as it may, regardless of your best exertion to keep away from them, challenges emerge and undermine your excursion; you should deal with them. Albeit troublesome, challenges do offer advantages.

Challenges drive you to take advantage of your innovativeness to concoct approaches to conquer them. The absolute best thoughts are considered when you're feeling the agonies of a test. Without the test, you couldn't ever have contemplated that innovative arrangement. At the point when obstructions hinder you, think about them as freedoms to discover innovative answers for overcome them.

Challenges advise you that you're human: you don't know it
all; you can't anticipate everything; you can't pull off
everything; you have impediments; you have shortcomings;
you commit errors. Difficulties advise you that you're delicate.
The fitting test can secure (or fix) you from getting prideful.
At the point when you need to beat various challenges to
arrive at your objective, you value your accomplishment even
more; these difficulties fill in as intensifiers for your
prosperity. Certain achievements wouldn't feel as important
on the off chance that they were less difficult. When
confronting difficulties, recollect that they're openings
that convey with them benefits: they require your
inventiveness, make you more grounded, keep you humble,
and enhance your accomplishments.

To develop actual fortitude, you should apply a touch of
protection from your mindset. Difficulties produce
obstruction, which creates inward guts. As you go through
difficulties, you become more grounded. Difficulties are a great
open door for development. They test your purpose and
obligation to your objectives. Also, when you conquer them,
you create passionate and mental strength.

3) She practices gratitude:

Gratitude resembles medication for the heart. It brings you euphoria, keeps you grounded and gives you a new point of view on life. An effective lady is thankful for what she has and doesn't underestimate anything since she realizes that nothing keeps going forever. Rehearsing thankfulness could be recording 10 things you're appreciative for or disclosing to yourself sure confirmations in the mirror every day. In any case, an effective lady cuts break of her day to consider what she's thankful for. According to a group of doctors, the feeling of gratitude has two phases:

First comes the affirmation of goodness in one's life. In a condition of appreciation, we say yes to life. We avow that all things considered, life is acceptable, and has components that make worth living, and wealthy in surface. The affirmation that we have gotten something satisfies us, both by its quality and by the exertion the provider put into picking it.

Second, appreciation is perceiving that a portion of the wellsprings of this integrity lie outside oneself. One can be thankful to others, to creatures, and to the world, however not to oneself. At this stage, we perceive the integrity in our lives and who to thank for it, ie., who made forfeits with the goal that we could be glad?

The two stages of gratitude comprise the recognition of the goodness in our lives, and then how this goodness came to us externally lies. By this process, we recognize the luck of everything that makes our lives —and ourselves— better.

GIVE THANKS

Here are the key findings from some of the researchers:

- A culture of gratitude assumes an essential part in the working environment: it predicts higher occupation fulfillment; Rehearsing appreciation at work causes the employees to feel more thankful about their work in general;

- Practicing gratitude at work isn't simply identified with present place of employment satisfaction, yet thankful employees additionally expect to be more happy with their positions in a half year's time;

- Employees who practice gratitude at work have a more grounded feeling of local area;

- Grateful practice will in general additional on the things they appreciate at work, as opposed to those that bother them.

Offering gratitude doesn't just influence the inside connections among partners and the executives. They can likewise improve the connection between the business and its clients, or fortify the trust between partners or financial backers.

Why Gratitude Works :

Gratitude is a magnanimous demonstration. Its demonstrations are done unequivocally, to show to individuals that they are valued. "A blessing that is unreservedly given" is one approach to comprehend what these demonstrations resemble.

For instance, in the event that somebody is tragic and you keep in touch with them a note of appreciation, you are likely not requesting something as a trade-off for this individual; all things considered, you are helping them to remember their worth, and offering thanks for their reality. Right now, you are not sitting tight for a "return note" from this individual.

In any event, when we don't anticipate a return, here and there they occur. Appreciation can be infectious, positively. In the past model, possibly when you are down, this individual will think of you a note as well. Here are two processes gratitude can influence:

1. Catharsis: is the cycle wherein an individual deliveries compelling feelings.

For instance, after a distressing or awful accident, crying gives a way to a particularly solid delivery, delivering the action soothing. Therapy works with appreciation.

To outline this, consider the blame related with "falling flat" to meet commitments. Maybe in the present circumstance, you would offer thanks to who you let down, trying to deliver that blame. The demonstrations are intended to pass on the appreciation that the companions have, regardless of a new frustration. Also, assets from passed friends and family may give a feeling of serenity that empowers the new proprietor to think about with appreciation that object and generally, that individual.

The utilization of appreciation fills in as a specialist of therapy, where the two people feel fulfilled eventually.

2. Reciprocity: as an idea from social brain science, is about the trading of activities. For this situation, it is about the trading of positive feeling. At the point when somebody plays out a demonstration of appreciation for someone else, thus, that individual might be spurred to accomplish something charitable for the previous individual or proceed with the kindness for an outsider. Envision having a feast with a companion, and they pleasantly request to pay for the excursion. You may object to and fro about parting the bill, however should they demand, you are probably going to feel thankful, and an all-encompassing obligation that the following feast is "your treat."

Generally, this is by and large how Reciprocity functions. In a sentimental relationship, the two accomplices make moves to satisfy the other one. This can evoke a few feelings like appreciation and obligation. A lot of effective women investigated these two feelings as a passionate reaction to a deliberately gave advantage.

Appreciation and obligation are related with the goal to compensate for the got advantage .It prompts inner inspiration and outside inspiration to respond.

4) She sets goals and she hunts them:

Have you contemplated what you need to do in five years' time? Is it true that you are clear about what your principle objective at work is right now? Do you understand what you need to have accomplished before the finish of today?

A successful lady understands what she needs throughout everyday life and how to get it. She defines objectives for herself and makes an activity intend to accomplish them. She estimates her prosperity, changes her arrangements as needs be, and afterward sets significantly more objectives. In the event that you need to succeed, you need to set objectives. Without objectives you need center and bearing. Objective setting not just permits you to assume responsibility for your life's course; it likewise gives you a benchmark to deciding if you are really succeeding. Consider the big picture: having 1,000,000 dollars in the bank is possibly evidence of achievement on the off chance that one of your objectives is to gather wealth. Assuming you will likely practice demonstrations of good cause, saving the cash for yourself is out of nowhere in opposition to how you would characterize achievement.

To achieve your objectives, notwithstanding, you need to realize how to set them in the beginning. You can't just say, "I need" and anticipate that it should occur. Objective setting is an interaction that begins with cautious thought of what you need to accomplish, and finishes with a ton of difficult work to really do it. In the middle, there are some all around characterized steps that rise above the points of interest of every objective. Realizing these means will permit you to figure objectives hat you can achieve.

1. Set Goals That Motivate You:

At the point when you set objectives for yourself, it is significant that they inspire you: this implies ensuring that they are imperative to you, and that there is an incentive in accomplishing them. On the off chance that you have little interest in the result, or they are unimportant given the bigger picture, at that point the odds of you placing in the work to get them going are thin. Inspiration is critical to accomplishing objectives.

Set objectives that identify with the high needs in your day to day existence. Without this kind of center, you can wind up with extremely numerous objectives, leaving you too brief period to dedicate to every one. Objective accomplishment requires responsibility, so to boost the probability of achievement, you need to feel a need to keep moving and have an "I should do this" demeanor. At the point when you don't have this, you hazard putting off what you need to do to make the objective a reality. This thus leaves you feeling baffled and disappointed with yourself, the two of which are de-propelling. Furthermore, you c an wind up in a ruinous "I can't do anything or be effective at anything" attitude.

Tip:

To ensure that your objective is motivating, record why it's significant and essential to you. Ask yourself, "If I somehow managed to impart my objective to other people, what might I advise them to persuade them it was a beneficial objective?" You can utilize this spurring esteem proclamation to help you in the event that you begin to question yourself or lose trust in your capacity to really make the objective occur.

2. Set SMART Goals:

You have presumably known about SMART objectives as of now. Be that as it may, do you generally apply the standard? The straightforward truth is that for objectives to be amazing, they ought to be intended to be SMART. There are numerous varieties of a big motivator for brilliant Here are our five brilliant principles of goal setting, introduced in this book:

- Specific.
- Measurable.
- Attainable.
- Relevant.
- Time Bound.

Set Specific Goals: Your goal should be clear and all around characterized. Ambiguous or summed up goals are pointless in light of the fact that they don't give adequate course. Keep in mind, you need goals to show you the way. Create it as simple as possible to get where you need to pass by characterizing correctly where you need to wind up.

Set Measurable Goals: Include precise amounts, dates, and so on in your goals so you can measure your degree of success. If your goal is simply defined as "To reduce expenses" how will you know when you have been successful? In one month's time if you have a 1 percent reduction or in two years' time when you have a 10 percent reduction? Without a way to measure your success you miss out on the celebration that comes with knowing you have actually achieved something.

Set Attainable Goals: Ensure that it's feasible to accomplish the objectives you set. On the off chance that you set an objective that you have no expectation of accomplishing, you will just unsettle yourself and disintegrate your certainty. Notwithstanding, fight the temptation to set objectives that are excessively simple. Achieving an objective that you didn't need to buckle down for can be paltry, best case scenario, and can likewise make you dread defining future objectives that convey a danger of non-accomplishment. By defining reasonable yet testing objectives, you hit the equilibrium you need. These are the kinds of objectives that expect you to "increase present expectations" and they bring the best close to home fulfillment.

Set Relevant Goals: Goals ought to be pertinent to the bearing you need your life and vocation to take. By keeping objectives lined up with this, you'll build up the center you need to excel and do what you need. Set broadly dissipated and conflicting objectives, and you'll waste your time – and your life – away.

Set Time-Bound Goals: Your goals should have a cutoff time. Once more, this implies that you know when you can praise achievement. At the point when you are chipping away at a cutoff time, your need to keep moving increments and accomplishment will come that a lot snappier.

5) She minimizes distractions:

Distractions just hold you back from remaining on target and zeroing in on your objectives. They redirect your consideration from t he main job, making you be less productive and motivated to complete things.

An effective lady knows this and takes care of interruptions during work hours. Now and again, that even includes denying responsibilities like social time with companions so she can complete her work.

That's how effective women maintain their success. They appear for themselves in each aspect of their life and aren't reluctant to say no when required. Regardless of whether they come as messages, emails, web-based media alarms or calls; a work colleague; or a brief glance online to watch news you've been following, distraction leads to a drain on your energy and your daily production.

With distractions regular in the work environment, it's nothing unexpected that all these little interferences affect organizations – however the degree might be more critical than you may might suspect. According to a group of entrepreneurs in the field of entrepreneurship, in UK the worker wastes 48 minutes per day on online interruptions alone (the number 1 is social media, with internet shopping following intently behind). This costs UK organizations an estimated 88$ billion every year in squandered hours. Distractions additionally make you bound to goof, with specialists at Michigan State University asserting that simply a 3-second interruption can twofold your danger of committing an error.

Be that as it may, distractions don't simply influence your work or your test modification; they can affect your enthusiastic wellbeing as well, causing pressure and low mind-set just and lower efficiency.

What can I do to avoid distractions?

Here are some of the ways you can avoid or reduce distractions:

-Set aside some time: On the off chance that you plan times to manage distractions like emails and social media in general, it might assist you with zeroing in on your work or studies even more successfully the remainder of the time. Preferably, pick an opportunity to manage distractions when you're normally less productive than usual – all things considered, you most likely understand what season of day you're acceptable at zeroing in on significant errands and when you think that its more hard to focus. On the other hand, you could relegate an hour toward the beginning and day's end to browse things like messages and messages, and make it a standard not to take a gander at them at some other time.

-Switch off your phone: The phone has become what should be complied – when it rings we feel constrained to respond to it, regardless of whether we're sincerely busy something significant. It might sound extreme, however take a stab turning your phone off when you're focusing on work or revising. Likewise let everyone around you realize that you will not be accepting insignificant calls between specific times.

-Avoid multitasking: Make a habit of working on 1 task at a time rather than dividing your attention between a variety of things you want to accomplish. Even if you have a long to-do list, you'll find you can get a lot more done if you finish 1 task before starting another. Make a list each morning of the things you want to work on in order of priority. Then set yourself a number of high-priority tasks to complete – don't just pick the smaller, easier tasks. Try not to feel tempted to start anything new until you've finished the task you're working on.

-Don't forget to take breaks : At the point when you have important work or study cutoff times approaching, make an effort not to work through without taking breaks.

You'll be much more beneficial on the off chance that you take normal brief breaks from your work area, with incidental longer breaks for lunch or a walk around in the outside air.

Taking a physical and mental break can help you concentrate even more viably when you get back to work or modifying, boosting your fixation and assisting you with feeling revived.

6) She prioritizes the most important tasks first:

Effective time management plays assumes a key in being successful. An effective lady realizes how to focus on so she can invest her energy on the main errands for the duration of the day. This smoothest out her work process, which makes everything stream even more easily and permits her to complete more. That way she can set aside a few minutes for what makes a difference most.

During the workday, errands are regularly focused on as per the necessities of others or the instantaneousness of cutoff times. This can occur in our own lives, as well, with restricted time spent on exercises that are significant, and more energy spent being "occupied with". Prioritizing errands viably—with expectation and as indicated by future objectives—can change this, guaranteeing that each undertaking you tackle drives worth and holding immaterial assignments back from jumbling your daily agenda.

Smart prioritization ordinarily includes making a plan, assessing assignments, and dispensing time and work to acquire the most worth a short measure of time. Prioritization ought to be adaptable, as you may have to interfere with low-need assignments for dire must-dos.

We found there are seven strategies for prioritizing tasks at work:

1. Have a list that contains all tasks in one: Effective prioritization comes from understanding the full extent of what you need to get done—even the most commonplace errands ought to be recorded and thought of. To give yourself a total picture, it's a smart thought to incorporate both individual and workday errands in a solitary assignment list.

Everything from getting your laundry to planning a one-on-one gathering with your manager ought to be caught in a similar spot. Whenever everything is recorded, prioritization normally occurs as indicated by the significance, direness, length, and prize of each assignment.

2. Identify what's important (Understanding your true goals): While it might seem like an immediate time management strategy, prioritization is key in achieving long-term goals. Understanding what you're really working toward—be it a promotion, a finished project, or a career change—helps you identify the tasks most pertinent to those future outcomes. It can be a good idea to break these larger goals into smaller, time-related goals. For example, a yearly goal can be deconstructed into monthly to-do lists, which then lead to weekly tasks, daily priorities, etc.

3. Highlight what's urgent: Your daily agenda ought to give full deceivability of cutoff times, assisting you with distinguishing which assignments should be finished expeditiously and to prepare as indicated by future cutoff times. Making cutoff times in any event, when they're not officially needed is likewise significant; else, you will keep pushing back significant errands basically in light of the fact that they aren't time-delicate. (This procedure can likewise be useful in expanding profitability and decreasing delaying).

4. Prioritize based on importance and urgency: The tasks should be categorized according to importance and urgency (and then prioritized):

- <u>Urgent and important:</u> These assignments ought to be done first.
- <u>Important but not urgent:</u> Block off time on your to-do list to get this done, without interruption.
- <u>Urgent but unimportant:</u> Delegate someone.
- <u>Neither urgent nor important:</u> Remove from your to-do list.

5. Avoid competing priorities: At the point when the undertakings you're dealing with aren't especially troublesome, it's generally simple to oversee them pair. Nonetheless, as trouble expands, research shows individuals who are in places of force are bound to focus on a solitary objective, while individuals in low positions will proceed to attempt to deal with numerous needs. This double assignment methodology has been connected to a decrease in execution, which implies the main undertakings aren't fulfilled to the best quality.

6. Consider effort: While gazing at a long to-do list, it's not difficult to get overpowered by the work that requirements doing—an inclination that diminishes efficiency and prompt s hesitation. A system to defeat this includes assessing undertakings as indicated by the exertion needed to finish them. On the off chance, that your plan for the day is getting excessively oppressive, focus on those errands that require negligible time and exertion and travel through them rapidly. This getting free from undertakings will give you some breathing space and produce a feeling of achievement to drive you for the duration of the day.

7. Review constantly and be realistic: Reviewing your task list and priorities is key in "regaining control and focus".

Tips for effective prioritization

As you understand the need of legitimate prioritization, it can out of nowhere feel more muddled—and more pressure instigating—than making a straightforward errand list.

The key methodologies referenced in this book, to help you set your priorities:

+ <u>Write everything down:</u> Individual and business tasks must be in one place.

+ <u>Evaluate long-term goals:</u> Think about your bigger long haul objectives, and the work you need to do to reach them.

+ <u>Break down large goals:</u> To see how to accomplish your long-term objectives, separate them into yearly, month to month, and week after week accomplishments.

+ <u>Create clear deadlines:</u> Give yourself full deceivability of deadlines, and create deadlines for yourself when none are officially required.

+ <u>Use the urgent-against important method:</u> Focus on earnest and significant undertakings; set a particular opportunity to chip away at significant nonurgent errands; and delegate or eliminate any remaining assignments.

+ <u>Create a daily to-do list:</u> Record three significant tasks that ought to be done that day. These relate ought to tasks identify with your bigger, future objectives.

+ <u>Avoid distractions:</u> Avoid competing tasks, e specially as the tasks difficulty increases.

7) She's financially savvy:

Financial stability gigantically affects your life and assumes a vital part in your future. A successful lady knows this and keeps steady over her funds with shrewd cash the executives. She is instructed on her funds, sees precisely where every last bit of her cash is coming from and isn't surprised when an unexpected bill pops up.

"Almost half of women—44%—are the essential providers in their families, and 27% of wedded ladies currently say they 'take control' of financial and retirement planning". This implies more ladies are controlling their own and family funds. Naturally, this makes ladies likewise answerable for their family's monetary achievement, so it is vital for ladies to be monetarily wise.

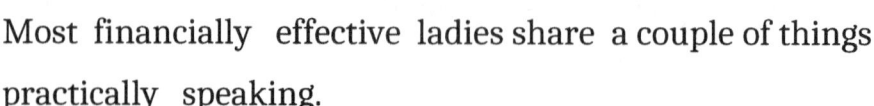

Most financially effective ladies share a couple of things practically speaking.

For one, they know where they stand monetarily. Also, they pay themselves first. Furthermore, they save. This control keeps up balance in the home and the spending plan in work. On the off chance that you are at present not a monetarily smart lady, make changes to your monetary propensities today. Utilize this book as a manual for kick you off.

+Do a Financial Check Up: Financially astute ladies know where they stand monetarily on the grounds that they do occasional monetary checkups. It's critical to realize the amount you procure, spend, save, and owe every month. In particular, set monetary objectives. Every month verify whether you are nearer to arriving at your reserve funds objectives. If not, sort out where your cash is proceeding to make course revisions. On the off chance that you owe a ton of obligation, set up an obligation take care of plan. At that point, every month track how much obligation you paid off and the amount you actually owe.

+ Set a Schedule to Track money and Pay Bills: Clever ladies are coordinated and may utilize a month to month spending plan to maintain their costs in control.

On the off chance that you don't have a spending plan, consider utilizing websites or application to help you track your buys and cover your bills. In my family, I handle the greater part of the accounts. To help our family stay coordinated, I track each bill's expected date on my iPhone schedule. I set an update alert the day preceding I might want to cover a bill. At that point, I set up programmed installments for those bills. I set bill dates as indicated by what is best for my family, and not founded on what's best for the companies. In the event that a due date for a bill is before your compensation day inquire as to whether you can change your installment due date. If not, consider excelling by one month on that specific bill, and afterward set up an installment plan that guarantees that the following bill is paid on the date you pick.

+ Set It and Forget It: In the event that you have a solid handle on your accounts, cover your bills naturally utilizing your bank's bill pay administration. Or then again you could set up programmed installments through the organization's sites. My solitary exemption for this standard is service bills.

You should take a gander at those month to month and focus on any potential spikes in utilization. There could be a water spill or mistaken meter perusing and you need to challenge these kinds of blunders right away. Every month, whenever you have affirmed the utility charges are exact, at that point take care of the bill. It doesn't make any difference if a lady is the family's provider or a similarly contributing stay-at-home mate. In any relationship the two players ought to be engaged with the funds. All ladies should know how the pay of their family is distributed, regardless of whether they are not covering the bills.

+ PAY YOURSELF FIRST: Financially sharp ladies pay themselves first by having programmed commitments made to retirement plan. Beginning from your first job—go all save for retirement by maximizing your yearly retirement reserve commitments. In the event that you start this training while you are youthful, your spending will get familiar with putting something aside for retirement first and at the most significant level conceivable. It is amazingly hard for some ladies to expand their retirement commitments once they start a family or increment their everyday costs.

In this way, figure out how to live off less, so you can save the most for retirement. For last year 2020, the IRS allows a representative to contribute up to $18,500 to her retirement account. Contrast this sum with what you are on target to save this year. In the event that your commitments will be under $18,500, perceive how close you can get to this figure and challenge yourself to offer more cash to your retirement store.

+ <u>Always Take Free Money:</u> In the event that you can't stand to maximize your yearly retirement commitments, you ought to at any rate put away sufficient cash to get the free cash (otherwise called the business match) offered by your manager. For instance, my boss will contribute up to five percent of my compensation to my retirement account, in the event that I contribute at any rate five percent of my compensation as well. In this way, on the off chance that I make $50,000 every year and contribute in any event $2,500 to my retirement, my boss will coordinate with my commitments with a $2,500 deposit into my retirement reserve. Inquire as to whether your organization offers a business coordinate and contribute in any event that rate to your retirement record to get the free cash.

<u>+ Don't Put All Your Eggs in One Basket:</u> You don't need to save the entirety of your retirement assets in a single spot. For those that qualify, at times it bodes well to invest resources into your boss asset to get your match commitments and afterward to place any additional cash into a Roth Individual Retirement Account (IRA). Roth IRAs are valuable since when you resign you can take out the cash tax exempt. In 2018, on the off chance that you are under 50 years of age you can contribute up to $5,500 each year into a Roth IRA. Pay directs who can add to a Roth IRA. Single individuals who need to add to a Roth IRA can't make more than $135,000, and on the off chance that you are hitched your consolidated pay can't surpass $199,000. Many single and wedded ladies don't fit the bill for Roth IRA for long on the off chance that they have significant compensations or a high joined family pay.

So on the off chance that you need to get the tax breaks of a Roth IRA do it while you are a making lower pay and are simply beginning in your vocation.

+ Save for when life is nice: It is recommended that you have three to a half year of everyday expenses kept for later.

You would prefer not to be monetarily disabled by a startling clinical cost, job loss, or disability. A huge reserve funds likewise guarantees that in the event that you need to return time off work to go to school, bring up youngsters, or seek after a lifelong change, you can settle on this choice without affecting your family's accounts. Monetarily smart ladies save routinely.

A strong bank account doesn't occur incidentally. The best activity is to set up programmed commitments into an investment account each time you get paid. Your finance office could put aside guide installments to your investment account or you could set up programmed moves from your bank to your bank account. You're checking and investment accounts don't need to be at a similar bank. Indeed, at times it's suggested the two records are isolated so you are not enticed to spend your investment funds on unnecessary things.

<u>+ Stay at Home Moms Can Save For Retirement Too:</u> In the event that you are a stay-at-home spouse, you additionally can have a retirement fund. Each time your life partner gets paid—so should you. Talk with a monetary consultant or bank about setting up a Spousal Individual Retirement Account (IRA). With this record, your companion can make commitments to a retirement account—in your name—on your benefit. Build revenue and time assist your cash with developing, so begin saving reliably as right on time as could be expected.

Monetarily effective ladies don't minimize their accomplishments, they realize that in case you're working effectively, your pay ought to mirror that, try not to allow anybody to exploit you, when purchasing goods or services, ensure you get a reasonable cost. On the off chance that you think a price is irrationally high, speak up and negotiate.

I get it – examining cash isn't simple. Being decisive doesn't come readily to most ladies. We are educated since the beginning that mentioning an increase in salary, bargaining at a superior cost, or requesting a superior advantages bundle is unfeminine, unladylike, or downright wrong. Yet, in the event that you need to get more richer, you need to begin arranging and negotiating.

On the off chance that you are going after a raise at work, do some research prior to putting forth your viewpoint:

- What do you bring to the company?
- What is the going rate for occupations in your sector?
- Is it the opportune chance to request a raise? (For instance, your chief is more averse to say "Yes" in the event that they are amidst a planning emergency.)

In case your organization can't expand your compensation, maybe you could haggle for different advantages like preparing openings and more holiday.

Financially effective ladies make an arrangement for their cash and stick to it.

+How much cash do you have in your present account?

+How much would you say you are saving and contributing?

+How much money do you have coming in consistently, and what amount do you save?

You can't oversee and make an arrangement for your funds in the event that you don't have the foggiest idea the amount you have. Information is power! A spending plan can assist you with seeing where your cash is going, know how much cash you have coming in consistently, where you can scale back your spending and the amount you can save every month.

We can't see into the future, yet it's almost certain that you'll need to manage crises every now and then. Save yourself from debt and obligation by building a contingency fund. In a perfect world, this will be identical to at any rate three months compensation.

Life isn't in every case nice. Awful things occur. You could lose your employment, your vehicle might die, Or you or one of your family gets sick.

Furthermore, on the off chance that you don't have a monetary buffer to count on it can bad situation worse.

Most Brits don't have the additional way to manage the unforeseen. A survey by Money Advice Service found that almost 50% of British grown-ups don't have more than 500$ in reserve funds.

Do you feel a flood of panic when you consider things turning out badly and not having the option to pay for it?

Nevertheless, imagine a scenario in which you could develop a practical secret stash in a half year.

8) She is constantly working on self-improvement:

An effective lady realizes that being sound works out positively past the physical and that psychological well-being is additionally vital. She rehearses self-consideration day by day, regardless of whether through contemplation, yoga, journaling, strolling, and so on, and is continually dealing with developing into a superior adaptation of herself. This permits her to clear her psyche, discover equilibrium and stay zeroed in on her objectives.

In reality, discovering approaches to learn and develop yourself doesn't need to occupy such a lot of time – and there numerous charming approaches to enhance your psyche for self-development.

Here are 8 personal development tips for busy women:

1)Ask more questions: Having a curious brain empowers you to get learn with a great deal each day, without particularly exertion. Posing inquiries causes, you access intriguing experiences that you would not have gone over something else – even in regions you think you know well. Questions are powerful in light of the fact that they can assist you with uncovering the examples of overcoming adversity of individuals you appreciate, and assist you with finding what inspires them. As you tune in to a companion or experienced mentor, you may track down that the information you get is exactly what you need to beat individual difficulties, advance in your vocation, or discover motivation for your own goals.

2)Look up words you don't know: Commonly we simply overlook words we're curious about – but rather there's such a lot of significant worth in   setting aside the effort to look through them up.   You'll accomplish more than improve your understanding perception – you'll likewise turn out to be more sophisticated in your composition and discourse.

3)Read a little each night: Talking about reading – you can fuse self-improvement into your every day schedule by doing a smidgen of reading before bed, in any event, for 15 minutes. Reading helps calm your mind and leave it with a nutritious thought before bed. On the off chance that you make perusing before bed a habit, you'll be stunned at the things you can learn just now before you sleep. The majority of the top books on self-awareness make extraordinary sleep time peruses in light of the fact that they depend on engaging stories and empowering guidance.

4)Sign up for newsletters: In case you're excessively occupied to continually investigate new wellsprings of information constantly, why not let the information come to you? Perhaps the simplest approaches to do this is by pursuing the newsletters and journals, including this book. Joining to a newsletter empowers you to consistently get little pieces of motivation or data that can assist you with improving different aspects of your life. It's an extraordinary method to get a consistent stream of fascinating material and set your learning on autopilot.

5)Learn from nature: Do you capitalize on time spent outside? Thinking about nature and finding tranquil minutes to intercede is a significant method to support self-improvement. Indeed, researchers have found that being in nature profoundly affects our cerebrums and conduct, and that time spent outside helps increment our consideration limit, creativity, and ability to connect with people. Participating in exercises like hiking, watching a nightfall, or taking a walk in a park can improve your mind-set and develop your appreciation for the straightforward delights throughout everyday life.

6)Learn from your mistakes: Probably the greatest approaches to consistently improve is to gain from your mixups. Since we're continually committing errors, there's no limit to the potential for personal growth. Individuals with intrapersonal insight are intelligent, and set aside effort to examine their musings and activities. Contemplating manners by which you might have better taken care of a circumstance will assist you with getting fulfilling brings about what's to come. Obviously, you would prefer not to wait on past encounters in a negative light, however acting naturally mindful can ensure you don't commit similar errors once more.

7)Create a vision board: Moving toward your goals from an innovative outlook can assist you with building up an affection for personal development. Making a dream board can help you channel your energy all the more beneficially and make a visual portrayal of your objectives. It likewise encourages you transform self-improvement into a continuous task, since it makes you set clear aims dependent on a way of life you need to accomplish. Albeit the way toward making a dream load up requires an underlying venture of time regarding arranging, after that it turns into a day-by-day token of your objectives and dreams.

8)Be patient: Last but not least, be patient to yourself. Try not to anticipate for the time being results. Creating yourself to arrive at your objectives is a progressive interaction, and everything thing you can manage to get results snappier is to stay persistent. Persistent is a critical layer of the well-known achievement icy mass that pushes you towards a daily existence you love. The more attentive you are, the more you'll find freedoms to learn, develop and improve. At that point, self-improvement will appear to be less similar to work and more like a delightful, deep-rooted attempt.

9) She makes health and exercise a priority:

Being solid isn't restricted to simply going to the rec center and eating right. It's an equilibrium of the whole self. It's a way of life that envelops our being and generally lifestyle.
An effective woman focuses on her wellbeing by feeding it with good food sources, exercise and normal self-care. This keeps her brain clear, engaged and profitable for the duration of the day. Regardless of whether it's running, doing yoga, going on a walk, writing in a diary, or scrubbing down,   effective ladies have a solid brain and body and comprehend that both are associated.

Long, tiring workday. Heavy traffic on the drive home. At the point when you at last arrive, you simply need to unwind, loosen up, and put another bustling day behind you.

That is what the majority of us need, without a doubt, however did you know there are more agreeable, more beneficial and better approaches to unwind a lot than slumping on the love seat and staring at the TV?

Getting into a customary exercise routine is unquestionably one of them. Certainly, exercise can seem as though more work, yet done right it can offer you a gigantic measure of delight and will leave you feeling more dynamic while giving you more energy for the following occupied day coming up.

Truth be told, putting every one of the chaotic parts of the day behind you and simply making the most of your activity routine — done at your own speed, such that suits you — will turn into an undeniably more viable approach to diminish pressure than just snatching the controller.

On the off chance that that isn't inspiration enough, here are a few hints for approaches to focus on wellness in your life — and to make the most of your way to arriving.

Here are five tips for how you can prioritize your health and fitness:

1- Try not to change everything at once: Pick a certain something and stick to it. It seems like we attempt to make a huge difference without a moment's delay - our weight, our relationship, our profession, our family and our accounts - as opposed to focus on. Yet, that approach is totally ridiculous. Indeed, once in a while the more we attempt to do, the less capable we are to make any of these changes, and everything endures.

So the initial step is to focus on is prioritize. Make a rundown of all that you need to change and what every thing on the rundown means for the other, and which bodes well to begin with. Orchestrate them arranged by significance. Presently take a gander at the principal thing on your rundown and set an unmistakable and feasible objective you realize you can achieve. Keep your rundown convenient and remind yourself every single day of your responsibility. You are currently on the pathway to progress, making each little stride in turn.

2- Plan to make a positive new habit, not simply an outcome:

Focus on the new conduct you need to accomplish, not the result. Let's assume you need to lose five kilos. The best approach to acquire this objective is by: Cleaning up your eating routine and getting very active. That is more powerful than simply zeroing in on the scale.

3- At the point when you slip, refocus rapidly:

There are times when we settle on decisions that we know are not good for us. We snatch that sweet pastry or skip a couple of days of our exercise. Probably the hardest activity is to excuse ourselves and move once again into our best practices straightaway. You don't have to overcompensate to attempt to fix the harm that was finished. This only makes getting back on track harder. Simply get once more into your sound daily schedule. Return to your little changes, back to your positive practices and right back to accomplishing that result.

4- Change your thinking: Your thoughts become your words, your words become your activities, your activities become your propensities, your propensities become your character. Add some certain speculation in this whole cycle, and the ultimate objective turns into your fate. On the off chance that you finish, you'll see that accomplishing your objective was probably the most straightforward thing you could possibly do on the grounds that you did it through little, attainable advances.

5- Do this process again: Use this process again and again to accomplish the objectives you spread out at the absolute starting point. Bit by bit, step by step, you will live your responsibilities and see the strength of your actual character. The reality is, there's no mystery ingredient, no handy solution. Obligation to growing great propensities over the long run IS the 'wizardry bullet'.

10) She is a morning person:

A habit that all effective women share is getting up right on time. This makes you substantially more profitable for the duration of the day. Your morning establishes the pace for the remainder of your day and permits your mind to stimulate before the evening. Effective ladies know this and utilize the morning for their potential benefit. Regardless of whether it's to plan or mash out projects before the forthcoming workday, the mornings are effective ladies' weapon for accomplishing more.

Being effective women means waking up early; or so we're constantly told. It makes you more productive. Successful people and CEOs do it. You'll be healthier and more joyful. You'll fee l in charge of your life.

On the off chance that rising early doesn't come naturally, there are a few procedures you can attempt. Early exercise and presenting yourself to light straightaway can help animate digestion and internal heat level, which makes you go all the more rapidly. There's been bunches of research about how a few group are naturally bound t o feel more ready in the first part of the day, while others are at their best around evening time. You may be more ready and have better psychological capacity in the early evening, for example. Indeed, a new report distributed in the diary Nature Communications gave additional proof that this is the situation. Taking a gander at information from more than 700,000 individuals, analysts found more than 350 hereditary elements that could impact whether individuals feel all the more normally stimulated either toward the beginning of the day or in the evening. The huge example size makes the examination the greatest of it's sort up until this point, however further exploration is expected to affirm the outcomes.

Along these lines, in the event that you don't normally feel alert toward the beginning of the day yet choose to get up early in any case, you might be sabotaging your actual peak performance times.  Obviously, individuals may have individual explanations behind making a early start.

"There might be different variables affecting everything, like excitement and high occupation fulfillment, which encourage energy to rise prior and will work," says Marilyn Davidson, professor emerita of work brain research at the University of Manchester. Parents with little youngsters or laborers with non-customary hours may likewise have no choice about what time they start the day.

How can an effective woman train herself to wake up on time in the morning?

Chances are you're not getting sufficient rest and need to change your sleep time schedule. On the off chance that a rest problem or other fundamental condition is to be faulted for your morning lethargy, there are treatments accessible, we'll cover the entirety of that and more here in this book so you can become one of those ladies morning.

Trouble getting up toward the beginning of the day isn't just about adoring your rest and hating mornings. Way of life factors, ailments, and medications can make it difficult to awaken. There are various things you can do to help you awaken. On the off chance that a fundamental condition is causing your exorbitant tiredness or languor in the first part of the day, you may require a blend of home cures and medical treatment.

Coming up next are tips and medicines that can help you to sleep better and awaken better:

Get on a sleep schedule: Going to bed and awakening simultaneously consistently is an absolute necessity on the off chance that you need to get on a decent rest timetable and train yourself to wake up early. Sort out how much rest you need — seven to nine hours out of each night is recommended — and plan to will be adequately early so you awaken feeling invigorated. Adhere to your sleep plan each day, including your days off, and your body will at last start awakening normally.

Improve your bedtime routine: You might be disrupting your endeavors to rise right on time without realizing it. Drinking caffeine the later piece of the day and utilizing gadgets that transmit blue light before bed can keep you from nodding off. To improve your sleep time schedule, take a stab at accomplishing something unwinding before bed, like reading or taking a warm bath. Keep away from exercises that've been appeared to meddle with your circadian cadence and cause sleeplessness, including: drinking alcohol before bed, spending too much time in bed during the day, drinking caffeine before bedtime and looking at screens, like phones and TV or laptop.

Eat better: Eating a sound eating routine expands your energy and encourages you sleep better. On the other side, food varieties that are for the most part thought to be unhealthy can cause you to feel sluggish and destroy your energy. Focus on an even eating routine brimming with food sources that increment your energy, like fruits and vegetables, whole grains, and food varieties high in omega-3 unsaturated fats.

Get regular exercise: Exercise has been demonstrated to improve sleep and conditions that can cause sleep deprivation and exorbitant sluggishness, like tension and sadness. It additionally expands energy levels by decreasing fatigue, remembering for individuals with conditions related with ongoing exhaustion.

Enjoy the daylight: Sunlight directs your circadian rhythms and improve your rest. If you get some sun first thing in the morning, it can help support your mind-set and energy levels for the remainder of the day. Take a stab at opening your blinds when you get up, having your espresso outside, or taking a short walk. You could likewise take a stab at laying down with your blinds open so you awaken to daylight.

<u>Get a sleep study:</u> In the event that you can't get up in the mornings subsequent to attempting different strategies or have seen sleep issue cautioning signs, converse with a doctor about a reference to a sleep trained professional. Taking an interest in a rest study can help analyze a sleep problem that might be at fault for your morning weakness.

Signs you may not be getting enough sleep: Experiencing difficulty getting up in the first part of the day is only one sign you're not getting sufficient rest. Here are some others: excessive yawning, irritability, lack of motivation, fatigue, excessive   daytime sleepiness, brain fog, increased appetite.

11) She dedicated time for getting her life organized:

A successful lady takes one day from the week for getting what fell behind – dishes, clothing, and so forth – and to prepare for the week ahead (arranging, supper preparing, and so on).

She's keeps steady over things, stays coordinated and keeps a clean climate. She realizes that a perfect climate hugely affects your psychological well-being which is the reason she does day by day errands to guarantee that her home and office are in every case very much kept. That way she has more opportunity to zero in on her most significant errands for the duration of the day.

12) She knows when to step away from work:

An effective lady realizes that there's a period for buckling down and afterward there's a period for loosening up following a long work day.

She realizes that work isn't all that matters, constantly, and that it's alright to make time to enjoy yourself.

Obviously, there will be days where she'll have to focus on work and that is alright, yet there will be likewise days for her to focus on self-care, and that is OK, as well.

13) She persevered in the face of adversity:

We as a whole have times where something terrible happens that kicks us in the gut, yet an effective lady doesn't allow anything to prevent her from following what she wants. She doesn't acknowledge disappointment, she doesn't let the heaviness of the world cut her down. All things considered, she follows what she needs with full power and pushes through until she dominates the competition. Like a phoenix finding new life, successful ladies don't break in the wake of misfortune, rather they only get that much stronger.

The Power of an Educated Woman: Education engages voice and organization. Instructed ladies create abilities, information and are engaged to guarantee their privileges. This permits them to settle on free and informed decisions. Low instructive achievement, for instance, is among the many intensifying components for being dependent upon oppressive conduct. Schooling can assume a basic part in moving standards and practices around abusive behavior at home to underscore prevention.

We should likewise not fail to remember that a significant obstruction to the accomplishment of value instruction for young ladies is the presence of sex based viciousness in and around schools. Parental worries about young ladies security in school and keeping in mind that making a trip to and from school seem to bring down female school enlistment in settings like South Asia, Africa and the Middle East.

This savagery incorporates lewd behavior, attack and tormenting executed by different understudies, out of school youth, instructors, school directors, and others. As indicated by South African information, teachers were the most well-known culprits of the assault of young ladies under age 15 (33% of cases).

14) She takes the initiative:

The expression "I can't" isn't even a piece of an effective lady's vocabulary. Regardless of whether she doesn't know precisely the thing she's doing, she still takes the initiative and gets things going in any case. She sorts it out, discovers answers for issues and doesn't yield to restricting convictions. She's a determined worker, a go-getter, and is consistently the first to hop up if a promising chance emerges.

Fortunately, initiative is an expertise that you can create, you can do this by following these steps:

1) Develop a Career Plan: Research has shown that women who have a drawn out long-term plan are bound to step up to the plate. Experts who understand what they need and where they need to go are undeniably bound to show initiative at work, particularly when the activity or choice will help them further their vocation objectives. Likewise, ensure that you comprehend your work, and your group and your association's motivation, so you understand what you ought to accomplish. When you understand what you need to accomplish, coordinate your vocation objectives with your own objectives, so you have something to pursue. (In your own life, the way to creating initiative is to define clear close to home objectives and afterward to work consistently towards accomplishing them).

2) Spot Opportunities and Potential Improvements:
Effective women who show initiative frequently do as such by spotting and following up on promising circumstances that their associates or pioneers have not taken note. They're interested about their association and how it functions, and they keep their brains open to groundbreaking thoughts and additional opportunities.

You ought to consistently be keeping watch for territories in your association that could utilize improvement. To spot openings and expected enhancements, consider the accompanying from the issue-discovering phase of the Simplex Process:

- What might our clients (inner and outer) need us to improve? What could they improve on the off chance that we could help them? How might we improve quality?
- Who else could we help by utilizing our center capabilities?
- What little issues do we have that could develop into greater ones?
- What slows our work or makes it more difficult? What do we frequently neglect to accomplish? Where do we have bottlenecks? What is frustrating and irritating to people on our team?

Start searching for these things – maybe set a rehashing arrangement in your journal to remind you to search for them; and, when things turn out badly, consider how you can fix them.

3) Sense-Check Your Ideas: Envision that you've concocted an inventive method of getting through a bottleneck in your client support measure. Before you head directly to your manager with your thought, pause and do some schoolwork.

Consider the expenses and dangers related with the thought. (Devices like Cost/Benefit Analysis, Risk Analysis and Impact Analysis will help here). Where the expense of the undertaking and the results of something turning out badly are little, consider proceeding with your thought straightforwardly, while keeping your manager "on top of it" (how far you ought to do this relies upon your relationship with your chief). Where dangers or expenses are huger, consider setting up a business case, and request approval before you go on. You've effectively shown activity by thinking of an answer. Ensure that you finish this by getting your work done on the thought. The more you have explored and thought about your thoughts, the higher your odds of progress will be.

4) Develop Rational Persistence: Persistence is the specialty of pushing ahead in any event, when you experience idleness or trouble. Individuals who show activity frequently experience troubles and misfortunes e n route, so versatility and normal perseverance (where you tune in to, consider, and fittingly adjust your heading relying upon others' information) are fundamental on the off chance that you need to accomplish what you've decided to do. At the point when you're persevering with your thought, you'll discover things a lot simpler in the event that you figure out how to oversee change viably – this can regularly have the effect among progress and disappointment for an undertaking. It's additionally useful to figure out how to open shut personalities, since individuals may as have now have an assessment regarding a matter before you even beginning introducing your thought.

5) Find Balance: While it's imperative to take initiative, it's similarly as critical to be astute in the manner that you use it. In certain circumstances, it tends to be improper to step up to the plate, and individuals who produce an excessive amount of additional work for others can agitate others.

For example, you may have worked with a partner who was "gung-ho" about each thought. He was continually pushing the group, and your chief, to lead the following undertaking or to carry out a novel thought. In any case, a portion of his thoughts were gullible, his perseverance in stepping up regularly went too far into forcefulness, and maybe the group felt that he "caused trouble" a lot when other colleagues were over-burden.

This is the reason it's so essential to learn great dynamic strategies. The more you improve these abilities, the better you'll be at deciding when a thought is acceptable, and it isn't. Thusly, you can build up a standing both for activity and for practical insight – a significant blend!

You'll additionally need to build up your passionate insight abilities. It's useful to realize how to peruse the feelings of others. This affectability can help you further choose when to step up to the plate, and when it's ideal to leave things alone.

6) Build Self-Confidence: It can take mental fortitude and a solid ability to be self-aware to show initiative, particularly on the off chance that you dread that individuals may differ with your initiatives or ideas. For example, set little objectives so you can accomplish some fast successes. What's more, drive yourself to do (positive) things that you'd in any case be frightened to do – this won't just assistance you fabricate your self-assurance, however it will help you construct the fortitude to achieve greater, more startling errands later on. This, alongside Visualization, can help you construct your self-assurance much further.

15) She surrounds herself with positive:

An effective ladies knows the force of encircle yourself with individuals who lift you up and support you. She just permits positive individuals in her day-to-day existence who persuade her to improve and rules out negative individuals who may hold her back. That way she can develop with individuals around her and gain from t heir encounters.

At the point when cheerful, positive colleagues surround you, the working day can pass abruptly of brotherhood. Partners can become companions, you appreciate coming to work, and you push each other to accomplish your best work. On the other hand, even a solitary day went through with a group that is negative, broken and cracked, you start to fear seeing similar inauspicious faces for every day. What's more, when there's no energy, thoughts evaporate and efficiency drops.

The solitary thing that will transform you, change your business, change your relationship, is that you should increase your expectations. Dispose of pessimistic individuals who bring you down. Encircle yourself with individuals who lift you up, loan you information and help you learn from your mistakes. Increase your expectations for your internal circle.

This concept is likewise called the law of attraction, and it returns in any event to Confucius in the sixth century BC, who thought of one of the primary statements about encircle yourself with great individuals: "Assuming you are the most brilliant individual in the room, you are in the wrong room." The possibility that you are who you encircle yourself with has kept going this long in light of the fact that it's actual – and you can utilize it to accomplish your fantasies in business and throughout everyday life.

Those you spend the most time with affect your states of mind, how you see the world and the assumptions you have of yourself. At the point when you encircle yourself with positive people, you're bound to embrace enabling convictions and consider life to be going on for you rather than to you.

Similarly, as you advantage when you encircle yourself with individuals who make you happy, you suffer when those in your business or groups of friends are negative or intolerant. **<u>Let go of negative relationships:</u>** Do you see yourself as a determined worker, yet your colleagues and group need desire? Is it true that you are looking for that next degree of achievement, yet are being kept down by people around you? Distinguishing individuals in your day-to-day existence who are cutting you down is the initial phase in making movements to your friend gathering or associates. Relinquishing negative relationships will permit you more opportunity to zero in on the positive ones. The most ideal approach to figure out who these people are is to consider how you feel after spending time with them. Do you have a positive outlook on yourself and prepared to take on new difficulties? Or then again do you feel agitated, uncertain of yourself and not in charge of your feelings? Our feelings exist to reveal to us things – they're a blessing that tells us what we need to change to feel more satisfied. In the event that you feel depleted, disturbed after spending time with someone, it's a sign they aren't beneficial for you.

It can regularly be awkward to back away from relationships that are inadequate. You would prefer not to sever ties, and you may have known a portion of these companions or partners for quite a while. Yet, it's fundamental not to feel committed in light of the fact that they are "old companions" or feel that you owe them something. Figure out what's driving your choice to remain in these connections, so you can change your attitude and free yourself. You'll be more set up to zero in on the main thing to you and your business.

<ins>Surround yourself with people who elevate you:</ins> We as a whole have objectives in our lives, however which goals are musts in your book? The pursuits you decide to put time in are an impression of your standards, as are your relationships. Is it accurate to say that you are attempting to develop your business? Provided that this is true, why might you decide to stay nearby individuals who bring pessimism and negativity into your life?

Possibly, you've quite recently become acclimated to having certain individuals around or are stressed over proceeding onward. Try not to allow dread to demolish your life.

At the point when you effectively decide to encircle yourself with individuals who make you upbeat and who share your aspirations, it lifts the norm of what you will or will not endure in your business and your life.

Surround yourself with people who are already successful: In the event that you need to speed up your success, it's essential to encircle yourself with individuals you can learn from. Join a genius gathering or discover somebody who is as of now getting the outcomes you need. They have a methodology for progress, if they know it, and by investing energy with them, you can build up a comparable one. How does this individual react to conflict? How do they network and forge relationships with key contacts? What propensities have they set up that lead to their significance? Notice their examples and perceive how you can adjust comparable ones into your life.

Surround yourself with people outside your comfort zone: All growth begins toward the finish of your usual comfort zone.

Ambitious women go to courses and workshops that feed their psyches and cause them to extend themselves. They open themselves to those with alternate points of view and constantly propel themselves out of their comfort zones. Hear from specialists and meet others such as yourself who are looking for the information expected to take their organizations to the following level. By bringing accomplishment into your life and going to Business Mastery, you not just addition openness to probably the most dedicated, driven individuals on the planet, however you perceive that your fantasies merit battling for. On the off chance that figuring out how to encircle yourself with great individuals is yet a test for you, work with a business mentor who can assist you with conquering restricting convictions and search out inspiring individuals to invest energy around. Not exclusively, will the mentor be a decent individual to invest energy with, they'll likewise have the option to assist you with recognizing which people in your day to day existence to restrict your openness to and help you search out new settings for producing valuable relationships.

The following time you question your road to success, investigate individuals around you. You are who you encircle yourself with, so quit bring your energy on individuals who carry you down with negative energy. Take all that concentration and move it to your new objective: figuring out how to encircle yourself with individuals who are positive, brilliant and supportive.

16) She's kind:

An effective lady knows the power of kindness and utilizations it. She realizes that being decent goes far in this world and has an effect on individuals around her. The old perspective on being savage to succeed is a distant memory. Effective ladies are liberal, generous while at the same time expecting nothing as a tradeoff. Generally, kindness is frequently viewed as a shortcoming in the realm of business. We would prefer not to quell the fire and extinguish the energy that drives us to accomplish, be fruitful, and move up stool of the corporate world. We can't be fruitful by turning over, taking a secondary lounge, and being non-fierce. At the point when we consider fruitful individual's consideration isn't the primary word that commonly comes into view. All that we are instructed through broad mass media demonstrates that kindness is something we use to get everything we might want.

It's in our unscripted TV dramas on TV and instilled in our unscrupulous legislative issues that it's the standard to say what individuals need to hear and afterward do what you like whenever you've acquired their trust. Kindness is a critical component to a fruitful, solid, mainstream, and healthy lifestyle. Kindness and strength are not totally unrelated – rather: just the solid can really be caring. Certified generosity isn't utilized to control. It's is given openly without assumption for return; in that lies strength. Kindness is something that we do on the grounds that we can, not on the grounds that we ought to. The basic dread is that we should imagine that we are something we are not or lose our characters during the time spent being caring. All things considered, who needs "they were pleasant" put on their gravestone?

Despite what might be expected, kindness can be that impetus that makes our character more compelling. It's not tied in with turning over and taking a rearward sitting effective. You can be decidedly confident inside the structure of kindness.

Thoughtfulness constructs trust and can be that extravagance seeing someone. In the business world, just transient reasoning permits those that climb in a consideration vacuum. Achievement is transient, on the off chance that it holds by any stretch of the imagination. Those that shun graciousness in Corporate America to make oodles of cash or to snatch brief increases don't construct establishments that last. Their workers aren't as faithful, connected with, nor are they amped up for being a piece of the association. It requires some investment to assemble trust, however just seconds to obliterate it. Whenever trust is addressed: your follow-boat will problematic too.

Studies show that, in opposition to our assumptions, the cream as a rule ascends to the top. Those top heads that become an enduring piece of a culture have been deliberate about building connections through trust, showing that they give it a second thought, and being benevolent with integrity. They comprehend that one doesn't get kind by doing kind things to other people. We do kind thing for others since we are kind and we do so paying little mind to the next individual's emotions toward us.

We are kind in light of the fact that it's the best activity. Do you recollect your parents saying: "don't sink to their level"? There is a fact in that saying and it's not simply a good old banality. We are not kind since we trust others will change – we are benevolent in light of the fact that it is correct. It's ideal to relinquish any need to feel response in benevolence (here's the strength part). We don't need to be cordial and well-disposed to individuals we believe are jerks, however it will do us no damage to be equitably kind. Consider it thusly: when you push against something and it pushes back – you will in general push harder, isn't that so? When you push against something and there's no opposition, you can't continue to push can you? Kindness isn't tied in with being an entryway tangle. You can be confident and immovably kind. You simply aren't giving any foothold to the pessimistic individual to continue to push. It's coming from a point of view of solidarity and not permitting others to push you out of your middle.

By permitting yourself to get disturbed or pulled down to a negative level in light of others activities, you have consequently given your power to them.

They presently own you. They control your feelings – not you. That is not clutching your own solidarity. You are presently moving to the tune of their music. Then again, when you stay focused, quiet, and grounded in thoughtfulness; really at that time are you genuinely in charge of yourself. It is tied in with being responsive refrains receptive. From a business point of view – would you rather advance somebody who is receptive and passionate or somebody who is focused, grounded, quiet, and mindfully responsive?

Envision what the world would resemble if everybody embraced the positive act of benevolence, even with individuals they couldn't help contradicting? Rather than being receptive, negative, passionate, and frequently irrational – we could be encircled by a steady, positive, insightful, responsive, and kind culture. Rather than seeing just the contemptuous and negative side of people being commended on TV; our kids would have legends to admire that exemplified human uprightness. Like waves in a lake or a surge from a cascade, thoughtfulness from one individual can extend and decidedly influence others around them. Maybe in any event, affecting society overall.

It's your decision: live as a reactive, emotional being or live as a kind, responsive being. At the point when you consider companions that you like to invest energy with or individuals that you admire, they presumably aren't contemptuous antagonistic individuals. Almost certainly, they are benevolent and smart. Achievement isn't just found in the corporate world – it begins at home. It begins with you. Nobody is too little to even consider having an effect so prevent thinking from an unimportance outlook and understand that you have more force than you might suspect. "Be kind and see your success happen".

17) She makes time for herself:

Although successful women are in need, they also know when it is time to relax and rejuvenate after a long day at work. You can't deal with every other person without dealing with yourself first, and an effective lady incorporates this. This could mean reflecting, journaling, doing yoga or going to another objective. The fact is that she perceives the significance of self-care and practices it every day.

Focusing in on your breathing, in any event, for five minutes, can assist you with venturing out of the Pressure that you're likely in and turns your parasympathetic nervous system on so you can rest. On the off chance that you need to keep it straightforward, breathe

in for the count of four and breathe out for the count of four.

Exchanging up your routine can help you step out of work mode and into unwinding. Anyway, rather than having supper at the table why not get it together and head down to the nearby park or your backyard? In the event that it's cold out, set up an excursion in your family room. There's nothing more unwinding than a decent cheese platter on a Friday night...

On the off chance that your week has left you feeling overpowered and run down, give yourself the endowment of a decent night's rest.

To set yourself up for a peaceful evening, an incredible science-supported hack is to have a sweltering shower and afterward rest in a cooled room.

Need to know why this functions admirably? During your hot shower, your veins in your skin will load up with blood (think about that pleasant blushing sparkle you have post hot shower or exercise).

At that point when you venture into the aircon, the quick drop in temperature will invigorate an inversion of that interaction – with blood hurrying from your limits to your essential organs.

The surge of blood to your crucial organs will place you in a condition of 'rest and digest', by actuating your parasympathetic nervous system, which is liable for long haul endurance.

There's nothing very like an endorphin rush to get your head out of the work mode and into a condition of unwinding. Regardless of whether you're a sprinter, a pilates-er or a CrossFit-a-holic, spending just 20 minutes in exercise mode will permit your body to deliver endorphins that will leave you feeling euphoric.

Another entrancing consequence of ordinary exercise is that it offers your body the chance to work on reacting to pressure. As indicated by gathering of specialists, a games and exercise therapist, normal exercise permits your body to smooth out correspondence between the frameworks associated with the pressure reaction. That is the reason the less dynamic we are, the more challenged we are when managing physical and emotional stress.

Ah, nature, getting out in nature has been appeared to positively affect your mind-set.

As per specialists in Cambridge Health Alliance, having something wonderful to zero in on like trees and greenery distract your mind from negative thinking, so your considerations become less loaded up with stress.

In the event that you can't quit considering the things you need to accomplish at work, get them out and onto paper. Compose a daily agenda or diary your contemplations for five minutes. This will give you the psychological clearness you need to unwind by getting every one of those work-put together contemplations down with respect to paper in an organized arrangement.

The best bit is it additionally offers you a chance to outwardly see your improvement as you tick things off when you're back in the workplace on Monday.

18) She communicates clearly:

Communication is a significant expertise that will benefit you regardless of what bearing you go throughout everyday life. A fruitful lady conveys unmistakably and isn't hesitant to express her thoughts. She converses with certainty and doesn't let the assessments of others burden her. Viable Communication is a critical part of accomplishment and an effective lady knows this, however tries this.

Successful correspondence is about something other than trading data. It's tied in with understanding the feeling and expectations behind the data. Just as having the option to plainly pass on a message, you need to likewise tune in such that acquires the full significance of what's being said and causes the other individual to feel heard and comprehended.

Effective communication seems like it ought to be intuitive. Nevertheless, generally very frequently, when we attempt to speak with others something roams. We say a certain something, the other individual hears something different, and misconceptions, disappointment, and clashes result. This can mess up your home, school, and work connections.

For a considerable lot of us, imparting even more plainly and viably requires acquiring some significant skills. Regardless of whether you're attempting to improve communication with your mate, children, chief, or colleagues, mastering these abilities can extend your associations with others, fabricate more noteworthy trust and regard, and improve cooperation, critical thinking and emotional health.

What's preventing you from communicating effectively?

- Stress and out-of-control emotion: At the point when you're focused or emotionally overwhelmed, you're bound to misread others, send confusing or off-putting nonverbal signals, and pass into unfortunate automatic patterns of conduct. To keep away from strife and misconceptions, you can figure out how to rapidly quiet down prior to proceeding with a discussion.

- Lack of focus: You can't impart adequately when you're performing multiple tasks. In case you're checking your telephone, arranging what you will say straightaway, you're practically sure to miss nonverbal signs in the discussion. To impart adequately, you need to maintain a strategic distance from interruptions and keep on track.

- Inconsistent body language: Nonverbal communication ought to support what is being said, not repudiate it. On the off chance that you say a certain something, yet your non-verbal communication says something different, your audience will probably feel that you're being unscrupulous. For instance, you can't say "yes" while shaking your head no.

- Negative body language: In the event that you can't help contradicting or you do not like what is being said, you may utilize antagonistic non-verbal communication to repel the other individual's message, like folding your arms, dodging eye to eye connection, or tapping your feet. You don't need to concur with, or even like what's being said, yet to impart successfully and not put the other individual on edge, it's imperative to try not to impart negative signs.

The skills that must be learned for the best effective communication make you able to easily persuade others:

Skills 1.Become an engaged listener :

When speaking with others, we frequently center around what we should say. Notwithstanding, effective communication is less about talking and more about listening. Listening great methods not simply understanding the words or the data being imparted, yet additionally understanding the feelings the speaker is attempting to pass on.

There's a major contrast between engaged listening and simply hearing. At the point when you truly listen—when you're engaged with what's being said—you'll hear the unobtrusive sounds in somebody's voice that reveal to you how that individual is feeling and the feelings they're attempting to convey. At the point when you're a drawn in audience, not exclusively will you better comprehend the other individual, you'll likewise cause that individual to feel heard and comprehended, which can help assemble a more grounded, deeper connection between you.

By communicating thusly, you'll additionally encounter an interaction that brings down pressure and supports physical and passionate prosperity. On the off chance that the individual you're conversing with is quiet, for instance, tuning in a connected way will assist with quieting you, as well. In addition, if the individual is upset, you can help quiet them by tuning in a mindful manner and causing the individual to feel comprehended. In the event that you will likely completely comprehend and associate with the other individual, tuning in a connected way will regularly fall into place. In the event that it doesn't, attempt the accompanying tips. The more you practice them, the seriously fulfilling and compensating your communications with others will turn into.

Tips for becoming an engaged listener:

+ Focus fully on the speaker: You can't listen in a connected manner in case you're continually checking your telephone or contemplating something different. You need to keep fixed on the occasion to-second involvement with request to get the inconspicuous subtleties and significant nonverbal signals in a discussion.

. In the event that you think that it's difficult to focus on certain speakers, take a stab at rehashing their words over in your mind—it'll build up their message and help you keep on track.

+ Favor your right ear: As weird as it sounds, the left half of the mind contains the essential handling places for both discourse appreciation and feelings. Since the left half of the cerebrum is associated with the right side of the body, preferring your right ear can help you better distinguish the enthusiastic subtleties of what somebody is saying.

+ Avoid interrupting or trying to redirect the conversation: By saying something like, "On the off chance that you imagine that is awful, allowed me to mention to you what befell me." Listening isn't equivalent to trusting that your turn will talk. You can't focus on the thing somebody's maxim in case you're framing what you will say straightaway. Frequently, the speaker can peruse your outward appearances and realize that your mind is somewhere else.

+ Show your interest in what's being said: Gesture at times, grin at the individual, and ensure your stance is open and welcoming. Urge the speaker to proceed with little verbal remarks like "yes" or "uh huh."

+ Try to set aside judgment: To discuss successfully with somebody, you don't need to like them or concur with their thoughts, qualities, or sentiments. Notwithstanding, you do have to put to the side your judgment and analysis to completely get them. The most difficult communication, when effectively executed, can regularly prompt an unlikely connection with somebody.

+ Provide feedback: On the off chance that there is disconnect, reflect what has been said by summarizing. "What I'm hearing is," or "Seems like you are saying," are incredible approaches to reflect back. Don't just recurrent what the speaker has said verbatim, however—you'll sound questionable or unintelligent. All things being equal, express what the speaker's words intend to you. Pose inquiries to explain specific focuses: "What do you mean when you say... " or "Is this what you mean?"

Skills 2.Pay attention to nonverbal signals

The manner in which you look, listen, move, and respond to someone else reveals to them more about how you're feeling than words alone at any point can.

Nonverbal correspondence, or non-verbal communication, incorporates outward appearances, body development and signals, eye-to-eye connection, act, the tone of your voice, and surprisingly your muscle pressure and relaxing.

Building up the capacity to understand and utilize nonverbal communication can assist you with associating others, express what you truly mean, explore challenging situations, and fabricate better connections at home and work.

- You can improve effective communication by utilizing open non-verbal communication—arms uncrossed, remaining with an open position or sitting as eager and anxious as can be, and keeping in touch with the individual you're conversing with.

- You can likewise utilize non-verbal communication to stress or upgrade your verbal message—applauding a companion while praising him on his prosperity, for instance, or beating your clench hands to underline your message.

Skill 3.Keep stress in check

How frequently have you felt focused on during a conflict with your life partner, kids, chief, companions, or associates and afterward said or accomplished something you later lamented? In the event that you can rapidly mitigate pressure and get back to a quiet state, you'll maintain a strategic distance from such laments, yet as a rule you'll additionally assist with quieting the other individual also. It's just when you're in a quiet, loosened up express that you'll have the option to know whether the circumstance requires a reaction, or whether the other individual's signs show it is smarter to stay quiet. In circumstances, for example, a job interview, business introduction, high-pressure meeting, or prologue to a friend or family member's family, it's important to manage your emotions to deal with your feelings, think and react quickly, and adequately convey under pressure.

Quick stress relief for effective communication: At the point when a discussion begins to get warmed, you need something fast to cut down the emotional intensity. By figuring out how to rapidly diminish pressure at the time, you can securely consider any compelling feelings you're encountering, control your sentiments, and carry on suitably.

-Recognize when you're becoming stressed: Your body will inform you as to whether you're stressed as you communicate. Are your muscles or stomach tight? Are your hands gripped? Is your breath shallow? It is safe to say that you are "neglecting" to breathe?

- Bring a second to quiet down prior to choosing to proceed with a discussion or defer it.

- Bring your senses to the rescue: The most ideal approach to quickly and dependably assuage pressure is through the senses—sight, sound, touch, taste, smell—or movement. For instance, you could pop a peppermint in your mouth, crush a pressure ball in your pocket, take a couple of full breaths, grip and loosen up your muscles, or just review a calming, tangible rich picture. Every individual reacts diversely to tactile info, so you need to discover a way of dealing with stress that is mitigating to you.

- Look for humor in the situation: At the point when utilized suitably, humor is an extraordinary method to alleviate pressure when communicating. When you or everyone around you begin viewing things too appropriately, figure out how to ease up the mind-set by sharing a joke or an interesting story.

- Be willing to compromise: Now and again, in the event that you can both curve a bit, you'll have the option to find a happy middle ground that diminishes the feelings of anxiety for everybody concerned. On the off chance that you understand that the other individual thinks often substantially more about an issue than you do, bargain might be simpler for you and a wise investment for the future of the relationship.

- Settle on a truce, if vital, and remove time from the circumstance so everybody can quiet down. Take a walk around if conceivable, or spend a few minutes meditating.

Skill 4.Assert yourself

Direct, self-assured articulation makes for clear communication and can help support your confidence and dynamic abilities. Being emphatic methods communicating your expressing, emotions, and necessities in a transparent way, while supporting yourself and regarding others. It doesn't mean being threatening, forceful, or requesting. Powerful communication consistently about understands the other individual, not tied in with winning a contention or compelling your sentiments on others.

To improve your assertiveness:

- **Value yourself and your choices:** They are just about as significant as anybody else's is.
- **Know your requirements and needs:** Learn to communicate them without encroaching on the rights of others.
- **Express negative thoughts in a positive manner:** It's OK to be irate, however you should stay deferential also.
- **Receive criticism emphatically:** Acknowledge praises generous, learn from your missteps, and request help when required.
- **Learn to say "no":** Know your cutoff points and don't allow others to exploit you, search for choices so everybody has a positive outlook on the result.

Skills 5.Developing assertive communication techniques
-Empathetic assertion passes on affectability to the next individual. To begin with, perceive the other individual's circumstance or emotions, at that point express your necessities or assessment. "I realize you've been exceptionally occupied at work, however I need you to set aside a few minutes for us also."

-Escalating assertion can be utilized when your first endeavors are not effective. You become progressively firm as time advances, which may incorporate laying out outcomes if your requirements are not met, for instance, "In the event that you don't comply with the agreement, I'll be compelled to seek after legitimate activity."

-Practice emphaticness in lower hazard circumstances to help develop your certainty, or then again inquire as to whether you can rehearse emphaticness methods on them first.

19) She loves the process more than the result:

An effective ladies doesn't let the dread of disappointment prevent her from accomplishing her objectives. She doesn't permit musings of self-uncertainty to enter her thoughts. She follows what she needs, gauges the dangers versus rewards, settles on a choice and pushes ahead with certainty.

How many women in this world do you know would like to have their own business? Be rich? Be famous? Travel the world?

It's not difficult to adore the result (being rich is superior to not being rich).

Be that as it may, more often than not you'll spend while in transit to accomplishing the following extraordinary thing will be spent battling. Overnight achievement is a legend. Battling is essential for it and, makes triumph much better.

Process is a higher priority than result... If process drives outcome, we may not realize where we're going, however we will realize we need to be there.

You need to adore the process more than you love the outcome. The outcome is here and there unclear in any case; the process is in your face each and every day. On the off chance that you can't love what you do on the everyday, you just will not arrive at your objective.

In the determined and aspiring society that we live in, all that we do is by all accounts estimated by the moment results. No more, are the days when we were educated to buckle down, stay steady and show restraint, to arrive at some degree of progress now it appears to be those standards are gradually getting out of date. Nevertheless, I am here to reveal insight into the significance of becoming hopelessly enamored with the process and not simply the outcomes.

It's an exercise that may fall off ridiculous from the outset, yet I challenge you to give this thought a tune in and apply it your everyday practice to perceive what results you get.

1-The Process Will Help Refocus Your Energy:

More often than not when we have a major hindrance toward us, after we gauge the difficulties of defeating the objective, we soon after fantasize about the outcomes. Briefly, we envision what's it going to feel like once we rout the difficulty and how the moment is going to look down to the littlest detail.

So centering and diverting your energy to zero in exclusively on the process is significant in light of the fact that the better you become simultaneously, the more you will appreciate the excursion and the outcomes. Have you at any point played a game for the first time and you were terrible in the beginning? Nevertheless, when you disregard the score, who's triumphant, and move your emphasis on the process to turn out to be better, you really begin to appreciate it more. At some point or another it doesn't make any difference who's triumphant in light of the fact that you're learning the process and improving outcomes.

In the event that you put all your energy and spotlight simply on the eventual outcomes while overlooking the process, you won't ever leave satisfied on the grounds that your bliss may be founded on the outcomes and not the process. Rehearsing the process isn't generally stylish, energizing or exciting, yet it will get you to where to need to be in the event that you figure out how to accept it.

2-The Process Makes You Pay Attention

The amazing thing about an process is it makes predictability. Each time you do stages 1, 2, and 3 you ought to get this outcome. This is the same old thing to us, yet so regularly we neglect. In the event that you study 30 mins consistently, the week prior to a test and you end up acing each test that implies you found a cycle that works for you. So understanding why we get the outcomes we get is similarly pretty much as significant as the actual outcomes. Nothing is seriously perplexing and unpleasant when we can't comprehend why something works or doesn't work.

3-The Process Makes You Appreciate the Results

Nothing causes you to value anything more than working and earning it, regardless of the amount we attempt to believe something else. At the point when we complete the pattern of defining an objective, pursuing it and finishing it, it gives us a sensation of approval that we can just get by putting forth the attempt. Presently envision getting anything, you needed without making the slightest effort or without applying any exertion and how unappreciative that would cause us to feel. I'm certain we can consider one individual who had a favored life and consistently got what he/she needed and from the external glancing in it seems like they had it made. Without realizing how to deal with disappointment or misfortunes, we will not ever value achievement when it introduces itself. Disappointments constrains us to focus and tells us we are drawing nearer to progress, however more significantly, it permits us to be careful and energetic about the process toward the end. The hardships that you will experience on your excursion through the interaction won't detract from your story, truth be told, it will significantly add meaning and purpose to it.

20) She's not afraid of failure:

A successful women doesn't let the dread of disappointment prevent her from accomplishing her objectives. She doesn't permit contemplations of self-uncertainty to enter her thoughts. She follows what she needs, gauges the dangers versus rewards, settles on a decision and pushes ahead with confidence.

It's critical to realize that in all that we do, there's consistently a possibility that we'll fizzle. Confronting that opportunity, and accepting it, isn't just gutsy – it likewise gives us a more full, more rewarding life.

Notwithstanding, here are a few ways to diminish the fear of falling:

- Analyze every single possible result – Many individuals experience dread of disappointment since they dread the unknown. Eliminate that dread by thinking about the entirety of the possible results of your choice.
- Learn to think all the more positively (As we talked earlier)– Positive reasoning is an inconceivably amazing approach to construct fearlessness and kill self-harm.
- Look at the worse case situation – sometimes, the direst outcome imaginable might be really shocking, and it could be entirely reasonable to fear disappointment. In different cases, notwithstanding, this most pessimistic scenario may really not be that awful, and perceiving this can help.
- Have an emergency course of action – If you're apprehensive about fizzling at something, having a "Plan B" set up can help you feel more sure about pushing ahead.

On the off chance that you fear disappointment, you may be uncomfortable defining goals.

However, objectives assist us with characterizing where we need to go throughout everyday life. Without objectives, we have no sure destination.

Numerous specialists suggest perception and visualization as an amazing asset for objective setting. Envisioning how life will be after you've arrived at your objective is an extraordinary help to keep you pushing ahead.

Angelina Nelson

2021 Angelina Nelson Publishing

www.ingramcontent.com/pod-product-compliance
Lightning Source LLC
Chambersburg PA
CBHW070357220526
45467CB00001B/409